Mel,
Thank you for
being a strong loving
leader to all, and me!
Maureen Mulcahey

Mel,
It has been
such a delight
in working with you
these past 2 years.
You have dedicated your
life to helping women and
the mission that has put before us.
Thank you for your love & support.
Vicki McQuillen

To

Mel Bonette

Mel,
You are an inspiration
to all of us. You are also
a beautiful special
person. We love you, Pat

June 1, 2000

From The P.W. Coordinating Team

Love to you, dear Mel.
Satisfaction and success in
the year ahead. Please —
let's keep in touch.
Always, Willie G.

He shall feed his flock like a shepherd:
He shall gather the lambs with his arms
and carry them in his bosom
and shall gently lead those that are
with young.

—Isaiah 40:11

Mel —
It's been a
pleasure to
serve on the
board with you.
I value your
friendship and
love! Love you
Ethelyn Vopel

Mel —
You've done a
terrific job. The
women of this church
will really come into
their own because of
you. Thanks a zillion.
Sue Neumann

YOU HAVE BEEN
A WONDERFUL
MODERATOR. IT HAS
BEEN A JOY AND
INSPIRATION TO
BE ON YOUR BOARD!
LOVE, Shirley

A Shepherd Looks at Psalm 23

ISBN 0-310-97776-2

All Scripture is from the King James Version.

Requests for information should be addressed to:

ZondervanPublishingHouse
Grand Rapids, Michigan 49530
http://www.zondervan.com

Senior Editor: Gwen Ellis
Project Editor: Judith Couchman
Designer: Big Cat Marketing Communications
Illustrations: Robert Sauber

Printed in China

00 01 02 /HK/ 3 2

A SHEPHERD LOOKS AT

Psalm 23

W. PHILLIP KELLER

CONTENTS

A Word from the Publisher

Once in a while a book is published the success of which surprises everyone. We then try to determine what happened to make that book work so well. Was it the author's passion for his topic? Was it his knowledge of the subject? Was it the audience's need for the material? Why do some books have such longevity? In the case of a book published more than thirty years ago by Zondervan Publishing House, it was all of these factors. *A Shepherd Looks at Psalm 23* captured the attention of the reading audience because Phillip Keller was a man who truly understood the meaning of the psalm. Keller, like the psalm writer David, had been a shepherd himself. He had lived among his sheep, protected them from harm, bathed their wounds, carried their young in his arms, and literally had laid down his life for them.

When Keller writes about cast sheep, we can see the poor helpless animal on its back in a ditch waiting for someone to right it so that it can walk again. When Keller talks about the shepherd making the sheep lie down in green pastures, we come to understand that sheep can only rest when they are free from fear, free from the torment of flies and other pests, and free from hunger. When sheep are well fed they will rest quietly, and it is the shepherd's task to see that they are well fed.

When we fully understand the relationship of a shepherd of the Middle East to his sheep, we can better understand the relationship of the Good

Shepherd to us, the sheep of His flock. We can then find the courage to trust our Shepherd, knowing that He has only our best interests at heart; understanding that He will never leave us nor forsake us even when we pass through the dark valleys of life.

We invite you to stop here for a while. To rest and read, and to feel the tender hand of the Good Shepherd resting upon your head as he cares for you.

The Publishers

INTRODUCTION

The Great Shepherd of the Soul

To a great extent the Bible is a collection of books written by men of humble origin, who penned it under the guidance of God's Spirit. Much of its terminology and teaching is couched in rural language, dealing with outdoor subjects and natural phenomena. The audience to whom these writings were addressed was for the most part simple, nomadic folk familiar with nature and the outdoor life of the countryside about them.

Divine revelation is irrevocably bound up with the basic subjects of the natural world. Our Lord Himself, when He was amongst us, continually used natural phenomena to explain supernatural truth in His parables. It is a sound, indisputable method, both scientifically and spiritually valid.

All this is understandable and meaningful when we recognize the fact that God is the author and originator of both the natural and supernatural (spiritual). The same basic laws, principles, and procedures function in these two contiguous realms. Therefore it follows that to understand one is to grasp the parallel principle in the other.

It must be stated here that it is through this type of scriptural interpretation that my own understanding of the Bible has become meaningful. This explains in part, why truths that I have shared with various audiences have been long remembered by them with great clarity.

Accordingly, I make no apologies for presenting this collection of "shepherd insights" into the well-known and loved—but often misunderstood—Twenty-third Psalm.

This book has been developed against a rather unique background which has perhaps given me an appreciation deeper than that of most men of what David had in mind when he wrote his beautiful poem.

I write as one who has had firsthand experience with every phase of sheep management.

First of all I grew up in East Africa, surrounded by simple native herders whose customs closely resembled those of their counterparts in the Middle East. I am thus intimately acquainted with the romance, the pathos, and the picturesque life of an Eastern shepherd. Second, as a young man, I actually made my livelihood for about eight years as a sheep owner and sheep rancher. Consequently, I write as one who has had firsthand experience with every phase of sheep management. Later, as the lay pastor of a community church, I shared the truths of this psalm, as a shepherd, with my "flock" every Sunday for several months.

It is, therefore, out of the variety of these firsthand experiences with sheep that the following chapters have emerged. To my knowledge this is the first time that a down-to-earth, hard-handed sheepman has ever written at length about the Shepherd's Psalm.

There is one difficulty that arises when writing a book based on a familiar portion of the Scriptures. One disillusions or disenchants the reader with some of his former notions about the psalm. Like much spiritual teaching the Twenty-third Psalm has had a certain amount of sentimental imagery wrapped around it with no sound basis in actual life. Some ideas advanced about it have, in fact, been ludicrous.

I would ask, then, that you, the reader, approach the pages that follow with an open mind and an unbiased spirit. If you do, fresh truth and exciting glimpses of God's care and concern for you will flood over your being. Then you will be brought into a bold, new appreciation of the endless effort put forth by our Savior for His sheep. Out of this there will then emerge a growing admiration and affection for The Great Shepherd of the Soul.

—W. *Phillip Keller, 1970*

PSALM 23

The LORD is my shepherd; I shall not want.

He maketh me to lie down in green pastures:
he leadeth me beside the still waters.

He restoreth my soul:
he leadeth me in the paths of righteousness
for his name's sake.

Yea, though I walk through the valley of the shadow of death,
I will fear no evil:
for thou art with me;
thy rod and thy staff they comfort me.

23

Thou preparest a table before me in the presence of mine enemies:
thou anointest my head with oil;
my cup runneth over.

Surely goodness and mercy shall follow me
all the days of my life:
and I will dwell in the house of the LORD for ever.

The LORD *is my shepherd,*
I shall not want.

The Lo my sh

The Lord Is My Shepherd

David, the author of this poem, himself a shepherd and the son of a shepherd, later to be known as the "Shepherd King" of Israel, stated explicitly, "The Lord is my Shepherd." To whom did he refer?

He referred to Jehovah, the Lord God of Israel.

His statement was confirmed by Jesus the Christ. When He was God incarnate amongst men, He declared emphatically, "I am the Good Shepherd."

So when the simple—though sublime—statement is made by a man or woman that "The Lord is my Shepherd," it immediately implies a profound yet practical working relationship between a human being and his Maker.

It links a lump of common clay to divine destiny—it means a mere mortal becomes the cherished object of divine diligence.

This thought alone should stir my spirit, quicken my own sense of awareness, and lend enormous dignity to myself as an individual. To think that God in Christ is deeply concerned about me as a particular person immediately gives great purpose and enormous meaning to my short sojourn upon this planet.

And the greater, the wider, the more majestic my concept is of Christ, the more vital will be my relationship to Him. Obviously, David, in this psalm, is speaking not as the shepherd, though he was one, but as a sheep, one of the flock. He spoke with a strong sense of pride, devotion, and admiration. It was as though he literally boasted aloud, "Look at who my shepherd is—my owner—my manager! The Lord is!"

After all, he knew from firsthand experience that the lot in life of any particular sheep depended on the type of man who owned it. Some men were gentle, kind, intelligent, brave, and selfless in their devotion to their stock. Others were not. Under one man sheep would struggle, starve, and suffer endless hardship. In another's care they would flourish and thrive contentedly.

God demonstrated at Calvary the deep desire of His heart to have men come under His benevolent care.

In Christ, God demonstrated at Calvary the deep desire of His heart to have men come under His benevolent care. He Himself absorbed the penalty for their perverseness, stating clearly that "All we like sheep have gone astray, we have turned every one to his own way, and the Lord hath laid on Him the iniquity of us all" (Isaiah 53:6).

Thus, in a very real and vital sense I truly belong to Him simply because

He has bought me again at the incredible price of His own laid-down life and shed blood.

Therefore He was entitled to say, "I am the good shepherd: the good shepherd giveth his life for the sheep" (John 10:11).

So there remains the moving realization that we have been bought with a price, that we are really not our own and He is well within His rights to lay claim upon our lives.

. . . .

I recall quite clearly how in my first venture with sheep, the question of paying a price for my ewes was so terribly important. They belonged to me only by virtue of the fact that I had paid hard cash for them. It was money earned by the blood, sweat, and tears drawn from my own body during the desperate grinding years of the depression. When I bought that first small flock I was buying them literally with my own body which had been laid down with this day in mind.

Because of this I felt in a special way that they were in very truth a part of me and I a part of them. There was an intimate identity involved which though not apparent on the surface to the casual observer, nonetheless made those thirty ewes exceedingly precious to me.

But the day I bought them I also realized that this was but the first stage in a long, lasting endeavor in which from then on, I would, as their owner, have to continually lay down my life for them if they were to flourish and prosper. Sheep do not "just take care of themselves," as some might suppose. They require, more than any other class of livestock, endless attention and meticulous care.

It is no accident that God has chosen to call us sheep. The behavior of sheep and human beings is similar in many ways. Our mass mind (or mob instincts), our fears and timidity, our stubbornness and stupidity, our perverse habits are all parallels of profound importance.

Yet despite these adverse characteristics Christ chooses us, buys us, calls us by name, makes us His own, and delights in caring for us.

It is this last aspect which is really why we are under obligation to recognize His ownership of us. He literally lays Himself out for us continually. He is ever interceding for us; He is ever guiding us by His gracious Spirit; He is ever working on our behalf to ensure that we will benefit from His care.

In fact, Psalm 23 might well be called "David's Hymn of Praise to Divine Diligence." For the poem goes on to recount the manner in which the Good Shepherd spares no pains for the welfare of His sheep.

Little wonder that the poet took pride in belonging to the Good Shepherd. Why shouldn't he?

I Shall Not Want

What a proud, positive, bold statement to make! Obviously, this is the sentiment of a sheep utterly satisfied with its owner, perfectly content with its lot in life.

Since the Lord is my Shepherd, I shall not want. Actually the word "want," as used here has a broader meaning than might at first be imagined. No doubt the main concept is that of not lacking—not deficient—in proper care, management, or husbandry.

But a second emphasis is the idea of being utterly contented in the Good Shepherd's care and consequently not craving or desiring anything more.

This may seem a strange statement for a man like David to have made if we think in terms only of physical or material needs. After all he had been hounded and harried repeatedly by the forces of his enemy Saul as well as those of his own estranged son Absalom. He was obviously a man who had known intense privation: deep personal poverty, acute hardship, and anguish of spirit.

It is imperative to keep a balanced view of the Christian life. To do this it is well to consider the careers of men like Elijah, John the Baptist, our Lord Himself—and even modern men of faith such as David

Livingstone—to realize that all of them experienced great personal privation and adversity.

When He was among us, the Great Shepherd Himself warned His disciples before His departure for glory that "in this world ye shall have tribulation: but be of good cheer; I have overcome the world" (John 16:33).

. . . .

"The Lord is my shepherd; I shall not want."

I am completely satisfied with His management of my life. Why? Because He is the sheepman to whom no trouble is too great as He cares for His flock. He loves them for their own sake as well as for His personal pleasure in them. He will, if necessary, be on the job twenty-four hours a day to see that they are properly provided for in every detail. Above all, He is very jealous of His name and high reputation as "The Good Shepherd."

He is the owner who delights in His flock. For Him there is no greater reward, no deeper satisfaction, than that of seeing His sheep contented, well fed, safe, and flourishing under His care. This is indeed His very "life." He gives all He has to it. He literally lays Himself out for those who are His.

He will go to no end of trouble and labor to supply them with the finest grazing, the richest pasturage, ample winter feed, and clean water. He will spare Himself no pains to provide shelter from storms, protection from ruthless enemies and the diseases and parasites to which sheep are so susceptible.

No wonder Jesus said, "I am the good shepherd: the good shepherd giveth his life for the sheep." And again, "I come that they might have life, and that they might have it more abundantly" (John 10:10).

From early dawn until late at night this utterly selfless Shepherd is alert to the welfare of His flock. For the diligent sheepman rises early and goes out first thing every morning without fail to look over his flock. It is the initial, intimate contact of the day. With a practiced, searching, sympathetic eye he examines the sheep to see that they are fit and content and able to be on their feet. In an instant he can tell if they have been molested during the night—whether any are ill or if there are some that require special attention.

He will spare Himself no pains to provide shelter from storms, protection from ruthless enemies and the diseases and parasites to which sheep are so susceptible.

Repeatedly through the day he casts his eye over the flock to make sure that all is well.

Nor even at night is he oblivious to their needs. He sleeps as it were "with one eye and both ears open," ready at the least sign of trouble to leap up and protect his own.

This is the sublime picture of the care given to those whose lives are under Christ's control. He knows all about their lives from morning to night.

"Blessed be the Lord, who daily loadeth us with benefits, even the God of our salvation" (Psalm 68:19).

"He that keepeth Israel shall neither slumber nor sleep" (Psalm 121:4).

*He maketh me lie down in green pastures:
he leadeth me beside the still waters.*

He mak

to lie

green p

He Maketh Me to Lie Down in Green Pastures

It is not generally recognized that many of the great sheep countries of the world are dry, semi-arid areas. Most breeds of sheep flourish best in this sort of terrain. They are susceptible to fewer hazards of health or parasites where the climate is dry. But in those same regions it is neither natural nor common to find green pastures. For example, Palestine where David wrote this psalm and kept his father's flocks, especially near Bethlehem, is a dry, brown, sunburned wasteland.

Green pastures did not just happen by chance. Green pastures were the product of tremendous labor, time, and skill in land use. Green pastures were the result of clearing rough, rocky land; of tearing out brush and roots and stumps; of deep plowing and careful soil preparation; of seeding and planting special grains and legumes; of irrigating with water and husbanding with care the crops of forage that would feed the flocks.

All of this represented tremendous toil, skill, and time for the careful shepherd. If his sheep were to enjoy green pastures amid the brown, barren hills it meant he had a tremendous job to do.

But green pastures are essential to success with sheep. When lambs are maturing and the ewes need green, succulent feed for a heavy milk flow, there is no substitute for good pasturage. No sight so satisfies the sheep owner as to see his flock well and quietly fed to repletion on rich, free forage, able to lie down to rest, ruminate, and gain weight.

A hungry, ill-fed sheep is ever on its feet, on the move, searching for another scanty mouthful of forage to try and satisfy its gnawing hunger. Such sheep are not contented, they do not thrive, they are no use to themselves nor to their owners. They languish and lack vigor and vitality.

In the Scriptures the picture portrayed of the Promised Land, to which God tried so hard to lead Israel from Egypt, was that of a "land flowing with milk and honey." Not only is this figurative language but also essentially scientific terminology. In agricultural terms we speak of a "milk flow" and "honey flow." By this we mean the peak season of spring and summer when pastures are at their most productive stages. The livestock that feed on the forage and the bees that visit the blossoms are said to be producing a corresponding "flow" of milk or honey. So a land flowing with milk and honey is land of rich, green, luxuriant pastures.

His concern for my care is beyond my comprehension, really. At best, all I can do is enjoy and revel in what He has brought into effect.

When God spoke of such a land for Israel, He also foresaw an abundant life of joy, victory, and contentment for His people.

. . . .

For the child of God, the Old Testament account of Israel moving from Egypt into the Promised Land is a picture of a people moving from sin into the life of overcoming victory. We are promised such a life. It has been provided for us and is made possible by the unrelenting effort of Christ on our behalf.

How He works to clear the life of rocks of stony unbelief. How He tries to tear out the roots of bitterness. He attempts to break up the hard, proud human heart that is set like sun-dried clay. He then sows the seed of His own precious Word, which if given half a chance to grow, will produce rich crops of contentment and peace. He waters this with the dews and rain of His own presence by the Holy Spirit. He tends and cares and cultivates the life, longing to see it become rich and green and productive.

This is all indicative of the unrelenting energy and industry of an owner who wishes to see his sheep satisfied and well fed. It all denotes my Shepherd's desire to see my best interests served. His concern for my care is beyond my comprehension, really. At best, all I can do is enjoy and revel in what He has brought into effect.

This life of quiet overcoming, of happy repose, of rest in His presence, of confidence in His management is something few Christians ever fully enjoy. Because of our own perverseness we often prefer to feed on the barren ground of the world around us. I used to marvel how some of my sheep actually chose inferior forage at times.

The Good Shepherd has supplied green pastures for those who care to move onto them and then find peace and plenty.

He Leadeth Me Beside the Still Waters

Although sheep thrive in dry, semi-arid country, they still require water. They are not like some of the African gazelles which can survive fairly well on the modest amount of moisture found in natural forage.

It will be noticed that here again the key or the clue to where water can be obtained lies with the shepherd. It is he who knows where the best drinking places are. In fact, very often he is the one who with much effort and industry has provided the watering places. And it is to these spots that he leads the flock.

But before thinking about the water sources themselves, we do well to understand the role of water in the animal body and why it is so essential for its well-being. The body of an animal such as a sheep is composed of about 70 percent water on an average. This fluid is used to maintain normal body metabolism; it is a portion of every cell, contributing to its turgidity and normal life functions. Water determines the vitality, strength, and vigor of the sheep and is essential to its health and general well-being.

If the supply of water for an animal drops off, bodily desiccation sets in. This dehydration of the tissues can result in serious damage to them. It can also mean that the animal becomes weak and impoverished.

An animal is made aware of water lack by thirst. Thirst indicates the need of the body to have its water supply replenished from a source outside itself.

Now, just as the physical body has a capacity and need for water, so Scripture points out to us clearly that the human personality, the human soul, has a capacity and need for the water of the Spirit of the eternal God.

When sheep are thirsty they become restless and set out in search of water to satisfy their thirst. If not led to good supplies of clean, pure water, they will often end up drinking from the polluted potholes, where they may pick up such internal parasites as nematodes, liver flukes, or gum disease germs.

In the same manner, Christ, our Good Shepherd, made it clear that thirsty souls of men and women can only be fully satisfied when their capacity and thirst for spiritual life is fully quenched by drawing on Himself.

The difficulty in all of this is that men and women who are "thirsty" for God (who do have a deep inner sense of searching and seeking; who are in quest of that which will completely satisfy) often are unsure of where to look or really what they are looking for. Their inner spiritual capacity for God and divine life is desiccated, and in their dilemma they will drink from any dirty pool to try and satisfy their thirst for fulfillment.

Saint Augustine of Africa summed it up well when he wrote, "O God! Thou hast made us for Thyself and our souls are restless, searching, 'til they find their rest in Thee."

. . . .

Most people are not aware that sheep can go for months on end, especially if the weather is not too hot, without actually drinking if there is a heavy dew on the grass each morning. Sheep, by habit, rise just before dawn and start to feed. Or if there is bright moonlight they will graze at night. The early hours are when the vegetation is drenched with dew, and sheep can keep fit on the amount of water taken in with their forage when they graze just before and after dawn.

The good shepherd, the diligent manager, makes sure that his sheep can be out and grazing on this dew-drenched vegetation. If necessary it will mean he himself has to rise early to be out with his flock. On the home ranch or afield he will see to it that his sheep benefit from this early grazing.

In the Christian life it is of more than passing significance to observe that those who are the most serene, most confident, and most able to cope with life's complexities often are those who rise early each day to feed on God's Word. It is in the quiet, early hours of the morning that they are led beside the quiet, still waters where they imbibe the very life of Christ for the day. This is much more than mere figure of speech. It is practical reality. The biographies of the great men and women of God repeatedly point out how the secret of the success in their spiritual life was attributed to the "quiet time" of each morning. There, alone, still, waiting for the Master's voice, one is led gently to the place where, as the old hymn puts it, "The still dews of His Spirit can be dropped into my life and soul."

Those who are the most serene, most confident, and most able to cope with life's complexities often are those who rise early each day to feed on God's Word.

In my mind's eye I can see my flock again. The gentleness, stillness, and softness of early morning always found my sheep knee deep in dew-drenched grass. There they fed heavily and contentedly. As the sun rose and its heat burned the dewdrops from the leaves, the flock would retire to find shade. There, fully satisfied and happily refreshed, they would lie down to rest and ruminate through the day. Nothing pleased me more.

I am confident that this is the same reaction in My Master's heart and mind when I meet the day in the same way. He loves to see me contented, quiet, at rest, and relaxed. He delights to know my soul and spirit have been refreshed and satisfied.

He restoreth my soul:
he leadeth me in the paths of righteousness
for his name's sake.

He res
my s

He Restoreth My Soul

Even David, the author of the psalm, who was much loved of God, knew what it was to be cast down and dejected. He had tasted defeat in his life and felt the frustration of having fallen under temptation. David was acquainted with the bitterness of feeling hopeless and without strength in himself.

In Psalm 42:11 he cries out, "Why art thou cast down, O my soul? and why art thou disquieted within me? hope thou in God: . . ."

Now there is an exact parallel to this in caring for the sheep. Only those intimately acquainted with sheep and their habits understand the significance of a "cast" sheep or a "cast down" sheep.

This is an old English shepherd's term for a sheep that has turned over on its back and cannot get up again by itself.

A cast sheep is a very pathetic sight. Lying on its back, its feet in the air, it flays away frantically, struggling to stand up, without success. Sometimes it will bleat a little for help, but generally it lies there lashing about in frightened frustration.

If the owner does not arrive on the scene within a reasonably short time, the sheep will die. This is but another reason why it is so essential for a careful sheepman to look over his flock every day, counting them to see that all are able to be up and on their feet. If one or two are missing, often the first thought to flash into his mind is, *One of my sheep is cast somewhere. I must go in search and set it on its feet again.*

It is not only the shepherd who keeps a sharp eye for cast sheep, but also the predators. Buzzards, vultures, dogs, coyotes, and cougars all know that a cast sheep is easy prey and that death is not far off.

This knowledge that a cast sheep is helpless, close to death, and vulnerable to attack makes the whole problem of cast sheep serious for the manager.

Nothing seems to arouse his constant care and diligent attention to the flock so much as the fact that even the largest, fattest, strongest, and sometimes healthiest sheep can become cast and be a casualty. Actually, it is often the fat sheep that are the most easily cast.

As a cast sheep lies there struggling, gases begin to build up in the rumen. As these expand they tend to retard and cut off blood circulation to extremities of the body, especially the legs. If the weather is very hot and sunny, a cast sheep can die in a few hours. If it is cool and rainy it may survive in this position for several days.

During my own years as a keeper of sheep, some of the most poignant memories are wrapped around the commingled anxiety of keeping a count of my flock and repeatedly saving and restoring cast sheep. It is not easy to convey on paper the sense of this ever-present danger. Often I would go out early and merely cast my eye across the sky. If I saw the black-winged buzzards circling overhead in their long, slow spirals, anxiety would grip me. Leaving everything else, I would immediately go out into the rough, wild pastures and count the flock to make sure every one was well and fit and able to be on its feet.

This is part of the drama depicted for us in the magnificent story of the ninety and nine sheep with one astray. There is the Shepherd's deep concern; His agonizing search; His longing to find the missing one; His delight in restoring it not only to its feet but also to the flock, as well as to Himself.

Some of the most poignant memories are wrapped around the commingled anxiety of keeping a count of my flock and repeatedly saving and restoring cast sheep.

Again and again I would spend hours searching for a single sheep that was missing. Then, more often than not, I would see it at a distance, down on its back, lying helpless. At once I would start to run toward it—hurrying as fast as I could—for every minute was critical. Within me there was a mingled sense of fear and joy; fear it might be too late; joy that it was found at all.

All of this is conveyed to my heart and mind when I repeat the simple statement, "He restoreth my soul!"

There is something intensely personal, intensely tender, intensely endearing, yet intensely fraught with danger in the picture. On the one hand there is the sheep, so helpless, so utterly immobilized, though otherwise so strong and healthy, and flourishing. On the other hand there is the attentive owner, quick and ready to come to its rescue, ever patient and tender and helpful.

It is important to point out that in the Christian life there is an exciting and comforting parallel here.

Many people have the idea that when a child of God falls, when he is frustrated and helpless in a spiritual dilemma, God becomes disgusted, fed up, and even furious with him.

This simply is not so.

One of the greatest revelations of the heart of God given to us by Christ is that of Himself as our Shepherd. He has the identical sensations of anxiety, concern, and compassion for cast men and women as I had for cast sheep. This is precisely why He looked on people with such pathos and compassion. It explains His magnanimous dealing with down-and-out individuals for whom even human society had no use. It reveals why He wept over those who spurned His affection. It discloses the depth of His understanding of undone people, to whom He came eagerly and quickly, ready to help, to save, to restore.

When I read the life story of Jesus Christ and examine carefully His conduct in coping with human need, I see Him again and again as the Good Shepherd, picking up cast sheep. The tenderness, the love, the patience that He used to restore Peter's soul after the terrible tragedy of his temptations is a classic picture of the Christ coming to restore one of His own.

And so He comes quietly, gently, reassuringly to me, no matter when or where or how I may be cast down.

He Leadeth Me in the Paths of Righteousness

The greatest single safeguard that a shepherd has in handling his flock is to keep them on the move. That is to say, they dare not be left on the same ground too long. They must be shifted from pasture to pasture periodically. This prevents overgrazing of the forage. It also avoids the rutting of trails and erosion of land from overuse.

In a word, there must be a predetermined plan of action, a deliberate, planned rotation from one grazing ground to another in line with right and proper principles of sound management. This sort of action is the idea David had in mind when he spoke of being led in paths of righteousness.

In this following of a precise plan of operation lies the secret for healthy land. Here is the key to successful sheep husbandry. The owner's entire name and reputation depend on how effectively and efficiently he keeps his charges moving onto wholesome, new, fresh forage. The one who directs his flock along this course is sure of success.

Casting my mind's eye back over the years that I kept sheep, no other single aspect of the ranch operations commanded more of my careful attention than the moving of the sheep. It literally dominated all my decisions. Not a day went by but what I would walk over the pasture in which the sheep were feeding to observe the balance between its growth and the grazing pressure upon it. As soon as the point was reached where I felt the maximum benefit for both sheep and land was not being met, the sheep were moved to a fresh field. On the average this meant they were put onto new ground almost every week.

If we are in earnest about wanting to do His will and to be led, He makes this possible by His own gracious Spirit, who is given to those who obey.

Coupled with this concept of management, there is, of course, the owner's intimate knowledge of his pastures. He has been all over his ground again and again. He knows its every advantage and every draw-back. He knows where his flock will thrive and he is aware of where the feed is poor. So he acts accordingly.

. . . .

Now as we turn to the human aspect of this theme we will be astonished at some of the parallels. As mentioned earlier, it is no mere whim on God's part to call us sheep. Our behavior patterns and life habits are so much like those of sheep it is well nigh embarrassing.

Scripture points out that most of us are a stiff-necked and stubborn lot. We prefer to follow our own fancies and turn to our own ways. "All we like sheep have gone astray; we have turned every one to his own way" (Isaiah 53:6). And this we do deliberately, repeatedly, even to our own disadvantage. There is something almost terrifying about the destructive self-determination of a human being. It is inexorably interlocked with personal pride and self-assertion. We insist we know what is best for us even though the disastrous results may be self-evident.

Turning to "my own way" simply means doing what I want. It implies that I feel free to assert my own wishes and carry out my own ideas. And this I do in spite of every warning.

In contrast to this, Christ the Good Shepherd comes gently and says, "I am the way, the truth, and the life: no man cometh unto the Father, but by me" (John 14:6).

The difficult point is that most of us don't want to come. We don't want to follow. We don't want to be led in paths of righteousness. Somehow it goes against our grain. We actually prefer to turn to our own ways even though it may take us straight into trouble.

Jesus never made light of the cost involved in following Him. In fact He made it painfully clear that it was a rugged life of self-denial. It entailed a whole new set of attitudes. It was not the natural, normal way a person would ordinarily live, and this is what made the price so prohibitive to most people.

Perhaps there are those who think He expects too much of us. Maybe they feel the demands are too drastic. Some may even consider His call impossible to carry out.

It would be if we had to depend on self-determination or self-discipline in order to succeed. But if we are in earnest about wanting to do His will and to be led, *He makes this possible* by His own gracious Spirit, who is given to those who *obey* (see Acts 5:32). For it is He who works in us *both* to *will* and *to do* His good pleasure (see Philippians 2:13).

Yea, though I walk through
the valley of the shadow of death,
I will fear no evil: for thou art with me;
thy rod and thy staff they comfort me.

Yea, Tho
Walk T
th

Yea, Though I Walk Through the Valley

Most of the efficient sheepmen endeavor to take their flocks onto distant summer ranges. This often entails long "drives." The sheep move along slowly, feeding as they go, gradually working their way up the mountains behind the receding snow. By late summer they are well up on the remote alpine meadows above timberline.

During this time the flock is entirely alone with the shepherd. They are in intimate contact with him and under his most personal attention day and night. And it is well to remember that this is done against a dramatic background of wild mountains, rushing rivers, alpine meadows, and high rangelands.

David, the psalmist, of course knew this type of terrain first-hand. When Samuel was sent of God to anoint him king over Israel, he was not at home with his brothers on the "home" ranch. Instead he was high up on the hills tending his father's flock. They had to send for him to come home. It is no wonder he could write so clearly and concisely of the relationship between a sheep and its owner.

He knew from firsthand experience about all the difficulties and dangers, as well as the delights, of the treks into high country. Again and again he had gone up into the summer range with his sheep. He knew this wild but wonderful country like the palm of his hand. Never did he take his flock where he had not already been. Always he had gone ahead to look over the country with care.

All the dangers of rampaging rivers in flood, avalanches, rock slides, poisonous plants, the ravages of predators that raid the flock, or the awesome storms of sleet and hail and snow were familiar to him. He had handled his sheep and managed them with care under all these adverse conditions. Nothing took him by surprise. He was fully prepared to safeguard his flock and tend them with skill under every circumstance.

As Christians we will sooner or later discover that it is in the valleys of our lives that we find refreshment from God Himself.

In the Christian life we often speak of wanting "to move onto higher ground with God." How we long to live above the lowlands of life. We want to get beyond the common crowd, to enter a more intimate walk with God. We speak of mountaintop experiences and we envy those who have ascended the heights and entered into this more sublime sort of life.

Often we get an erroneous idea about how this takes place. It is as though we imagined we can be "airlifted" onto higher ground. On the rough trail of the Christian life this is not so. As with ordinary sheep management, so with God's people: one gains higher ground by climbing up through the valleys.

. . . .

Every mountain has its valleys. Its sides are scarred by deep ravines, gulches, and draws. The best route to the top is always along those valleys.

Any sheepman familiar with the high country knows this. He leads his flock gently but persistently up the paths that wind through the dark valleys. Not only is this the way of the gentlest grades, but also it is the well-watered route. Here one finds refreshing water all along the way. There are rivers, streams, springs, and quiet pools in the deep defiles.

As Christians we will sooner or later discover that it is in the valleys of our lives that we find refreshment from God Himself. It is not until we have walked with Him through some very deep troubles that we discover He can lead us to find our refreshment in Him right there in the midst of our difficulty. We are thrilled beyond words when there comes restoration to our souls and spirits from His own gracious Spirit.

Another reason the rancher chooses to take his flock into the high country by way of the valleys is that this is generally where the richest feed and best forage is to be found.

The flock is not hurried. There are lambs along that have never been this way before. The shepherd wants to be sure there will be not only water but also the best grazing available for the ewes and their lambs. Generally the choicest meadows are in these valleys along the stream banks. Here the sheep can feed as they move toward the high country.

Naturally these grassy slopes are often on the floor of steep-walled canyons and gulches. There may be towering cliffs above them on either side. The valley floor itself may be in dark shadow, with the sun seldom reaching the bottom except for a few hours around noon.

The shepherd knows from past experience that predators like coyotes, bears, wolves, or cougars can take cover in these broken cliffs and from their vantage point prey on his flock. He knows these valleys can be subject to sudden storms and flash floods that send walls of water rampaging down the slopes. There could be rock slides, mud or snow avalanches, or a dozen other natural disasters that would destroy or injure his sheep. But in spite of such hazards, he also knows that this is still the best way to take his flock to the high country. He spares himself no pains or trouble or time to keep an eye out there for any danger that might develop.

Our Shepherd knows all of this when He leads us through the valleys. He knows where we can find strength, sustenance, and gentle grazing despite every threat of disaster about us.

It is a most reassuring and reinforcing experience to the children of God to discover that there is, even in the dark valley, a source of strength and courage to be found in God. It is when we can look back over life and see how the Shepherd's hand has guided and sustained us in the darkest hours that our faith is renewed.

Thy Rod and Thy Staff They Comfort Me

In the Middle East the shepherd carried only a rod and staff. Some of my most vivid boyhood recollections are those of watching the African herdsmen shepherding their stock with only a long, slender stick and a rough *knob-kerrie* in their hands. These are the common and universal equipment of the primitive sheepman.

The rod was an extension of the owner's own right arm. It stood as a symbol of his strength, his power, his authority in any serious situation. The rod was what he relied on to safeguard both himself and his flock in danger. It was, furthermore, the instrument he used to discipline and correct any wayward sheep that insisted on wandering away.

Because of this, the sheep asserts that the owner's rod, his weapon of power, authority, and defense, is a continuous comfort to him. For with it the manager is able to carry out effective control of his flock in every situation.

The rod speaks, therefore, of the spoken Word, the expressed intent, the extended activity of God's mind and will in dealing with men. It implies the authority of divinity. It carries with it the convicting power and irrefutable impact of *"Thus saith the Lord."*

Just as for the sheep of David's day there was comfort and consolation in seeing the rod in the shepherd's skillful hands, so in our day there is great assurance in our own hearts as we contemplate the power, veracity, and potent authority vested in God's Word. For, in fact, the Scriptures are His rod. They are the extension of His mind and will and intentions to mortal man.

Another interesting use of the rod in the Shepherd's hand was to examine and count the sheep. In the terminology of the Old Testament this was referred to as passing "under the rod" (see Ezekiel 20:37). This meant not only coming under the owner's control and authority, but also being subject to his most careful, intimate, and firsthand examination.

The picture is a very poignant one. As each animal comes out of the corral and through the gate, it is stopped by the shepherd's outstretched rod. He opens the fleece with the rod; he runs his skillful hands over the body; he feels for any sign of trouble; he examines the sheep with care to see that all is well. This is a most searching process, entailing every intimate detail. It is, too, a comfort to the sheep, for only in this way can its hidden problems be laid bare before the shepherd.

This is what was meant in Psalm 139:23–24 when the psalmist wrote, "Search me, O God, and know my heart: try me, and know my thoughts: And see if there be any wicked way in me, and lead me in the way everlasting."

This is a process from which we need not shrink. It is not something to avoid. It is done in concern and compassion for our welfare. The Great Shepherd of our souls has our own best interests at heart when He so searches us. What a comfort this should be to the child of God, who can trust in God's care.

Finally, the shepherd's rod is an instrument of protection both for himself and his sheep when they are in danger. It is used as both a defense and a deterrent against anything that would attack.

The skilled shepherd uses his rod to drive off predators such as coyotes, wolves, cougars, or stray dogs. Often it is used to beat the brush, discouraging snakes and other creatures from disturbing the flock. In extreme cases, such as David recounted to Saul, the psalmist no doubt used his rod to attack the lion and the bear that came to raid his flocks.

It was the rod of God's Word that Christ, our Good Shepherd, used in

His own encounter with that serpent—Satan—during His desert temptation. It is the same Word of God that we can count on again and again to counter the assaults and attacks of Satan. And it matters not whether the guise He assumes is that of a subtle serpent or a roaring lion that desires to destroy us.

In every situation and under every circumstance there is comfort in the knowledge that God's Word can meet and master the difficulty if we will rely on it.

. . . .

In a sense the staff, more than any other item of his personal equipment, identifies the shepherd as a shepherd. No one in any other profession carries a shepherd's staff. It is designed, shaped, and adapted especially to the needs of sheep. And it is used only for their benefit.

The staff is essentially a symbol of the concern, the compassion, that a shepherd has for his charges. No other single word can better describe its function on behalf of the flock than that it is for their *comfort*.

Whereas the rod conveys the concept of authority, of power, of discipline, of defense against danger, the word "staff" speaks of all that is long-suffering and kind.

Just as the rod of God is emblematic of the Word of God, so the staff is symbolic of the Spirit of God. In Christ's dealings with us as individuals there is the essence of the sweetness, the comfort and consolation, the gentle correction brought about by the word of His gracious Spirit.

There are three areas of sheep management in which the staff plays a most significant role. The first of these lies in drawing sheep together into an intimate relationship. The shepherd will use his staff to gently lift a newborn lamb and bring it to his mother if they are separated. He does this because he does not wish to have the ewe reject her offspring if it bears the odor of his hands upon it.

In every situation and under every circumstance there is comfort in the knowledge that God's Word can meet and master the difficulty if we will rely on it.

But in precisely the same way, the staff is used by the shepherd to reach out and catch individual sheep, young or old, and draw them close to himself for intimate examination. The staff is very useful this way for the shy and timid sheep that normally tend to keep at a distance from the shepherd.

The staff is also used for guiding sheep. Again and again I have seen a shepherd use his staff to guide his sheep gently into a new path through some gate, or along dangerous, difficult routes. He does not use it actually to beat the beast. Rather, the tip of the long, slender stick is laid gently against the animal's side and the pressure applied guides the sheep in the way the owner wants it to go. Thus the sheep is reassured of its proper path.

Sometimes I have been fascinated to see how a shepherd will actually hold his staff against the side of some sheep that is a special pet or favorite, simply so that they "are in touch." They will walk along this way almost as though they were "hand in hand." The sheep obviously enjoys this special attention from the shepherd and revels in the close, personal, intimate contact between them. To be treated in this special way by the shepherd is to know comfort in a deep dimension. It is a delightful and moving picture.

In our walk with God we are told explicitly by Christ Himself that it will be His Spirit who would be sent to guide us and to lead us into all truth (see John 16:13). This same gracious Spirit takes the Truth of God, the Word of God, and makes it plain to our hearts and minds and spiritual understanding. It is He who gently, tenderly, but persistently says to us, "This is the way—walk in it." And as we comply and cooperate with His gentle prompting a sense of safety, comfort, and well-being envelops us.

It is when I do not do this that I end up in difficulty. It is then that I find myself in a jam of some sort. And here again the gracious Spirit comes to my rescue, just as the shepherd rescued his sheep out of the situations into which their stupidity led them. A common occurrence was to find sheep stuck fast in labyrinths of wild roses or brambles where they had pushed in to find a few stray mouthfuls of green grass. Soon the thorns were so hooked in their wool they could not possibly pull free, tug as they might. Only the use of a staff could free them from their entanglement.

Likewise with us. Many of our jams and impasses are of our own making. In stubborn, self-willed, self-assertion we keep pushing ourselves into situations from which we cannot extricate ourselves. Then in tenderness, compassion, and care, our Shepherd comes to us. He draws near and in tenderness lifts us by His Spirit out of the difficulty and dilemma. What patience God has with us! What long- suffering and compassion! What forgiveness!

Thy staff comforts me! Your Spirit, O Christ, is my consolation!

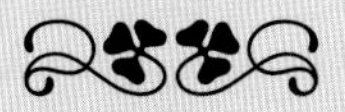

Thou preparest a table before me in the presence of mine enemies: thou anointest my head with oil; my cup runneth over.

Thou Pr
a tabl
Be

Thou Preparest a Table Before Me

In some of the finest sheep country of the world, especially in the Western United States and southern Europe, the high plateaus of the sheep ranges are referred to as "mesas"—the Spanish word for tables.

So it may be seen that what David referred to as a table was actually the entire high summer range. Though these "mesas" may be remote and hard to reach, the energetic and aggressive sheep owner takes the time and trouble to ready them for the arrival of his flocks.

Early in the season, even before all the snow has been melted by spring sunshine, he will go ahead and make preliminary survey trips into this rough, wild country. He will look it over with great care, keeping ever in mind its best use for his flock during the coming season.

Then, just before the sheep arrive, he will make another expedition or two to prepare the table land for them. He will take along a supply of salt and minerals to be distributed over the range at specific posts for the benefit of the sheep during the summer. The intelligent, careful manger will also decide well ahead of time where his camps will be located so the sheep will have the best bed grounds. He will go over the range carefully to determine how vigorous the grass and upland vegetation are. At this time he will decide which glades and basins can be used only lightly and which slopes and meadows may be grazed more heavily.

He will check to see if there are poisonous weeds appearing, and if so, he will plan his grazing program to avoid them, or take drastic steps to eradicate them.

Unknown to me, the first sheep ranch I owned had a rather prolific native strand of both blue and white cammas. The blue cammas were a delightful sight in the spring when they bloomed along the beaches. The white cammas, though a much less conspicuous flower, were also quite attractive but a deadly menace to sheep. If lambs, in particular, ate or even just nibbled a few of the lily-like leaves as they emerged in the grass sward during Spring, it would spell certain death. The lambs would become paralyzed, stiffen up like blocks of wood, and simply succumb to the toxic poisons from the plants.

Consequently, my youngsters and I spent days and days going over the ground, plucking out these poisonous plants. It was a recurring task that was done every spring before the sheep went on these pastures. Though tedious and tiring with all the bending, it was a case of "preparing the table in the presence of mine enemies." If my sheep were to survive, it simply had to be done.

All of this sort of thing was in the back of David's mind as he penned these lines. I can picture him walking slowly over the summer range ahead of his flock. His eagle eye is sharp for any signs of poisonous weed, which he will pluck before his sheep get to them. No doubt he had armfuls to get rid of for the safety of his flock.

. . . .

Like sheep, and especially lambs, we somehow feel that we have to try everything that comes our way. We have to taste this thing and that, sample everything just to see what it's like. And we may very well know that some things are deadly. They can do us no good. They can be most destructive. Still, somehow, we give them a whirl anyway.

To forestall our getting into grief of this sort, we need to remember that our Master has been there ahead of us coping, with every situation that would otherwise undo us.

Another task the attentive shepherd takes on in the summer is to keep an eye out for predators. He will look for signs and spoor of wolves, coyotes, cougars, and bears. If these raid or molest the sheep he will have to hunt them down or go to great pains to trap them so that his flock can rest in peace.

Often what actually happens is that these crafty ones are up on the rimrock, watching every movement the sheep make, hoping for a chance to make a swift, sneaking attack that will stampede the sheep. Then one or another of the flock is bound to fall easy prey to the attacker's fierce teeth and claws.

The picture here is full of drama, action, suspense—and possible death. Only the alertness of the sheepman who tends his flock on the tableland in full view of possible enemies can prevent them falling prey to attack. It is only his preparation for such an eventuality that can possibly save the sheep from being panicked and slaughtered by their predators.

At all times we would be wise to walk a little closer to Christ. This is one sure place of safety.

Again we are given a sublime picture of our Saviour, who knows every wile, every trick, every treachery of our enemy Satan and his companions. Always we are in danger of attack. Scripture sometimes refers to him as a "roaring lion" who goes about seeking whom he may devour.

At all times we would be wise to walk a little closer to Christ. This is one sure place of safety. It is always the distant sheep, the roamers, the wanderers, that are picked off by the predators in an unsuspecting moment. Generally the attackers are gone before the shepherd is alerted by their cry for help. Some sheep, of course, are utterly dumb with fear under attack; they will not even give a plaintive bleat before their blood is spilled.

The same is true of Christians. Many of us get into deep difficulty, beyond ourselves; we are stricken dumb with apprehension, unable even to call or cry out for help; we just crumple under our adversary's attack.

But Christ is too concerned about us to allow this to happen. Our Shepherd wants to forestall such a calamity. He wants our summer sojourn to be in peace. Our Lord wants our mountaintop times to be tranquil interludes. And they will be if we just have the common sense to stay near Him where He can protect us. Read His Word each day. Spend some time talking to Him. We should give Him opportunity to converse with us by His Spirit as we contemplate His life and work for us as our Shepherd.

Thou Anointest My Head with Oil

In the terminology of the sheepman, "summertime is fly time." By this, reference is made to the hordes of insects that emerge with the advent of warm weather. Only those people who have kept livestock or studied wildlife habits are aware of the serious problems for animals presented by insects in the summer.

Sheep are especially troubled by the nose fly, or nasal fly, as it is sometimes called. These little flies buzz about the sheep's head, attempting to deposit their eggs on the damp mucous membranes of the sheep's nose. If they are successful, the eggs will hatch in a few days to form small, slender, wormlike larvae. These work their way up the nasal passages into the sheep's head; there they burrow into the flesh and set up an intense irritation accompanied by severe inflammation.

For relief from this agonizing annoyance sheep will deliberately beat their heads against trees, rocks, posts, or brush. They will rub them in the soil and thrash around against woody growth. In extreme cases of intense infestation a sheep may even kill itself in a frenzied endeavor to gain respite form the aggravation. Often advanced stages of infection from these flies will lead to blindness.

Because of this, when the nose flies hover around the flock, some of the sheep will become frantic with fear and panic in their attempt to escape their tormentors. They will stamp their feet erratically and race from place to place in the pasture trying desperately to elude the flies. Some may run so much they will drop from sheer exhaustion. Others may toss their heads up and down for hours. They will hide in any bush or woodland that offers shelter. On some occasions they may refuse to graze in the open at all.

All of this excitement and distraction has a devastating effect on the entire flock. Ewes and lambs rapidly lose condition and begin to drop in weight. The ewes go off milking and their lambs stop growing gainfully. Some sheep may be injured in their headlong rushes of panic; others may be blinded and some even killed outright.

Only the strictest attention to the behavior of the sheep by the shepherd can forestall the difficulties of "fly time." At the very first sign of flies among the flock he will apply an antidote to their heads. I always preferred to use a homemade remedy composed of linseed oil, sulphur, and tar, which I smeared over the sheep's nose and head as a protection against nose flies.

What an incredible transformation this would make among the sheep. Once the oil had been applied to the sheep's head there was an immediate change in behavior. Gone was the aggravation; gone the frenzy; gone the irritability and the restlessness. Instead, the sheep would start to feed quietly again, then soon lie down in peaceful contentment.

This, to me, is the exact picture of irritation in my own life. How easy it is for there to be a fly in the ointment of even my most lofty spiritual experience! So often it is the small, petty annoyances that ruin my repose. It is the niggling distractions that become burning issues that can well nigh drive me round the bend or up the wall. At times some tiny, tantalizing thing torments me to the point where I feel I am just beating my brains out. And so my behavior as a child of God degenerates to a most disgraceful sort of frustrated tirade.

Just as with the sheep there must be continuous and renewed application of oil to forestall the "flies" in my life, there must be a continuous anointing of God's gracious Spirit to counteract the ever-present aggravation of personality conflicts. Only one application of oil, sulphur, and tar was not enough for the entire summer. It was a process that had to be repeated. The fresh application was the effective antidote.

There are those who contend that in the Christian life one need only have a single, initial anointing of God's Spirit. Yet the frustrations of daily dilemmas demonstrate that one must have Him come continuously to the troubled mind and heart to counteract the attacks of one's tormentors.

This is a practical and intimate matter between me and my Master. In Luke 11:13 Christ Himself, our Shepherd, urges us to speak for the Holy Spirit to be given to us by the Father.

It is both a logical and legitimate desire for us to have the daily anointing of God's gracious Spirit upon our minds. God alone can form in us the mind of Christ. The Holy Spirit alone can give to us the attitudes of Christ. He alone makes it possible for us to react to aggravations and annoyances with quietness and calmness.

. . . .

But summertime is more than just fly-time. It is also "scab-time." Scab is an irritating and highly contagious disease common among sheep the world over. Caused by a minute, microscopic parasite that proliferates in warm weather, "scab" spread throughout the flock by direct contact between infected and non-infected animals.

Sheep love to rub heads in an affectionate and friendly manner. Scab is often found most commonly on the head. When two sheep rub together, the infection spreads readily from one to the other.

In the Old Testament when it was declared that the sacrificial lambs should be without blemish, the thought uppermost in the writer's mind was that the animal should be free of scab. In a very real and direct sense, scab is significant of contamination of sin, of evil.

It is both a logical and legitimate desire for us to have the daily anointing of God's gracious Spirit upon our minds. God alone can form in us the mind of Christ.

Again, as with the flies, the only effective antidote is to apply linseed oil, sulphur, and other chemicals that can control this disease. In many sheep-rearing countries, dips are built and the entire flock is put through the dip. Each animal is completely submerged in the solution until its entire body is soaked. The most difficult part to dip is the head. The head has to be plunged under repeatedly to insure that scab located there will be controlled. Some sheepmen take great care to treat the head by hand.

In the Christian life, most of our contamination by the world, by sin, by that which would defile and disease us spiritually, comes through our minds. It is a case of mind meeting mind to transit ideas, concepts, and attitudes that may be damaging.

Often it is when we "get our heads together" with someone else who may not necessarily have the mind of Christ that we come away imbued with concepts that are not Christian.

Often the mass media, which are largely responsible for shaping our minds, are in the control of men whose characters are not Christlike; who in some cases are actually anti-Christian.

One cannot be exposed to such contacts without coming away contaminated. Here again, the only possible, practical path to attaining a mind free of the world's contamination is to be conscious daily, hourly, of the purging presence of God's Holy Spirit, applying Himself to our minds.

There are those who seem unable to realize His control of their minds and thoughts. It is a simple matter of faith and acceptance. Just as one asks Christ to come into one's life initially to assure complete control of one's conduct, so one invites the Holy Spirit to come into one's conscious and subconscious mind to monitor one's thought life. Just as by faith we believe and know and accept and thank Christ for coming into our lives, so by simple faith and confidence in the same Christ, we believe and know and accept with thanks the coming (or anointing) of His gracious Spirit upon our minds. Then, having done this, we simply proceed to live and act and think as He directs us.

My Cup Runneth Over

Autumn days can be golden under Indian summer weather. No other season finds them so fit and well and strong. No wonder David wrote, "My cup runneth over."

But at the same time, unexpected blizzards can blow up or sleet storms suddenly shroud the hills. The flock and their owner can pass through appalling suffering together.

It is here that I grasp another aspect altogether of the meaning of a cup that overflows. There is in every life a cup of suffering. Jesus Christ referred to His agony in the Garden of Gethsemane and at Calvary as His cup. And had it not overflowed with His life poured out for men, we would have perished.

In tending my sheep I carried a bottle in my pocket containing a mixture of brandy and water. Whenever a ewe or lamb was chilled from undue exposure to wet, cold weather I would pour a few spoonfuls down its throat. In a matter of minutes the chilled creature would be on its feet and full of renewed energy. It was especially cute the way the lambs would wiggle their tails with joyous excitement as the warmth from the brandy spread through their bodies.

The important thing was for me to be there on time, to find the frozen, chilled sheep before it was too late. I had to be in the storm with them, alert to every one that was in distress. Some of the most vivid memories of my sheep ranching days are wrapped around the awful storms my flock and I went through together. I can see again the gray-black banks of storm clouds sweeping in off the sea; I can see the sleet and hail and snow sweeping across the hills; I can see the sheep racing for shelter in the tall timber; I can see them standing there soaked, chilled, and dejected. The young lambs, especially, went through appalling misery, without the benefit of a full, heavy fleece to protect them. Some would succumb and lie down in distress, only to become more cramped and chilled.

Then it was that my mixture of brandy and water came to their rescue. I'm sure the Palestinian shepherds must have likewise shared their wine with their chilled and frozen sheep.

What a picture of my Master, sharing the wine, the very lifeblood of His own suffering, from His overflowing cup, poured out at Calvary for me. He is there with me in every storm. My Shepherd is alert to every approaching disaster that threatens His people. He has been through the storms of sufferings before. He bore our sorrows and was acquainted with our grief.

Now, no matter what storms I face, His very life and strength and vitality are poured into mine. They overflow so that the cup of my life runs over with His life . . . often with great blessing and benefit to others who see me stand up so well in the midst of trials and suffering.

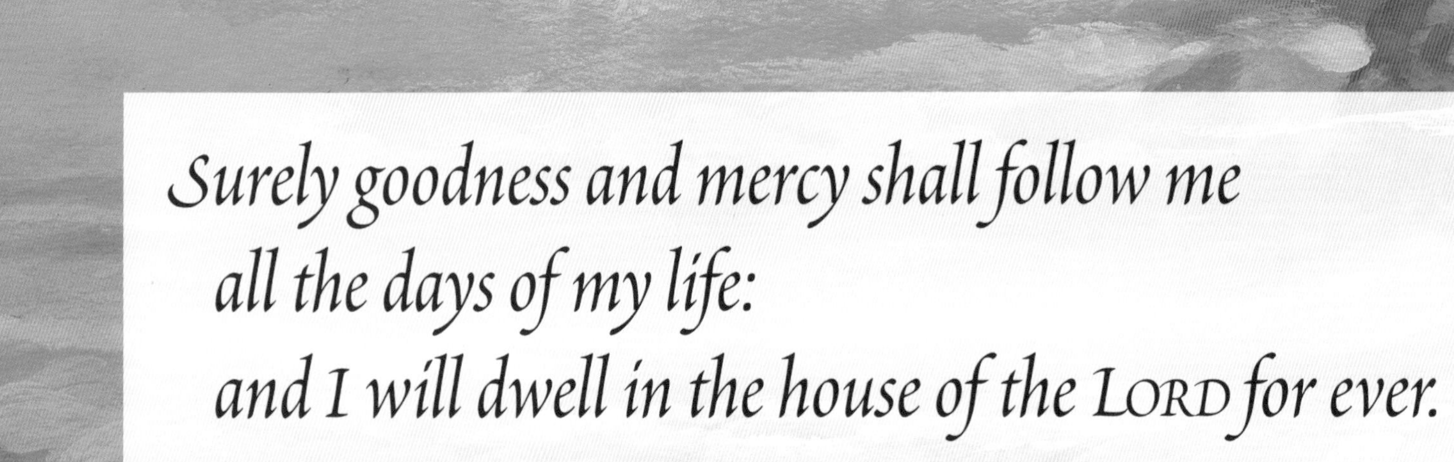

Surely goodness and mercy shall follow me
all the days of my life:
and I will dwell in the house of the LORD *for ever.*

Surely Go
and M
Shall Fo

Surely Goodness and Mercy Shall Follow Me

Throughout the study of this psalm, continuous emphasis has been put upon the care exercised by the attentive sheepman. It has been stressed how essential to the welfare of the sheep is the rancher's diligent effort and labor. All the benefits enjoyed by a flock under skilled and loving management have been drawn in bold lines.

Now all of this is summed up here by the psalmist in one brave but simple statement: "Surely goodness and mercy shall follow me all the days of my life."

The sheep with such a shepherd knows of a surety that his is a privileged position. No matter what comes, at least and always he can be perfectly sure that goodness and mercy will be in the picture. He reassures himself that he is ever under sound, sympathetic, intelligent ownership. What more need he care about? Goodness and mercy will be the treatment he receives from his master's expert, loving hands.

Not only is this a bold statement, but it is somewhat of a boast, an exclamation of implicit confidence in the One who controls his career and destiny.

How many Christians actually feel this way about Christ? How many of us are truly confident that, no matter what occurs in our lives, we are being followed by goodness and mercy? Of course it is very simple to speak this way when things are going well. If my health is excellent, my income is flourishing, my family is well, and my friends are fond of me it is not hard to say "Surely goodness and mercy shall follow me all the days of my life."

But what about when one's body breaks down? What do I say when I stand by helplessly, as I have had to do, and watch a life partner die by degrees under appalling pain? What is my reaction when my job folds up and there is no money to meet bills? What happens if my children can't make their grades in school or get caught running with the wrong gang? What do I say when suddenly, without good grounds, friends prove false and turn against me?

These are the times that test a person's confidence in the care of Christ. These are the occasions when the chips are down and life is more than a list of pious platitudes. When my little world is falling apart and the dream castle of my ambitions and hopes crumbles into ruins, can I honestly declare, "Surely—yes, surely goodness and mercy shall follow me all the days of my life"? Or is this sheer humbug and a maddening mockery?

. . . .

In looking back over my own life, in light of my own love and care for my sheep, I can see again and again a similar compassion and concern for me in my Master's management of my affairs. There have been events that at the time seemed like utter calamities; there have been paths down which He led me that appeared like blind alleys; there have been days He took me through that were well nigh black as night itself. But in the end it all turned out for my benefit and my well-being.

With my natural tendencies to fear, worry, and ask "why," it was not always easy to assume that He really did know what He was doing with me.

With my limited understanding as a finite human being I could not always comprehend that His management was executed in infinite wisdom. With my natural tendencies to fear, worry, and ask "why," it was not always easy to assume that He really did know what He was doing with me. There were times I was tempted to panic, to bolt, and to leave His care. Somehow I had the strange, stupid notion that I could survive better on my own.

Despite this behavior, I am so glad He did not give up. I am so grateful He did follow me in goodness and mercy. The only possible motivations were His own love, His care and concern for me as one of His sheep. And despite my doubts, despite my misgivings about His management of my affairs, He picked me up and bore me back again in great tenderness.

In retrospect I realize that for the one who is truly in Christ's care, no difficulty can arise, no dilemma emerge, no seeming disaster descend on life without eventual good coming out of the chaos. This is the goodness and mercy of my Master in my life. It has become the great foundation of my faith and confidence in Him.

I love Him because He first loved me.

His goodness, mercy, and compassion to me are new every day. And my assurance is lodged in these aspects of His character. My trust is in His love for me as His own. My serenity has as its basis an implicit, unshakable reliance on His ability to do the right thing, the best thing in any given situation.

This to me is the supreme portrait of my Shepherd. Continually there flow out to me His goodness and His mercy, which, even though I do not deserve them, come unremittingly from their source of supply—His own great heart of love.

Herein is the essence of all that has gone before in this psalm.

All the care, all the work, all the alert watchfulness, all the skill, all the concern, all the self-sacrifice are born of His love—the love of One who loves His sheep, loves His work, loves His role as a Shepherd.

He looks on my life in tenderness, for He loves me deeply. He sees the long years during which His goodness and mercy have followed me without slackening. He longs to see some measure of that same goodness and mercy not only passed on to others by me, but also passed back to Him with joy.

He longs for love—my love.

And I love Him—only and because He first loved me.

Then He is satisfied.

I Will Dwell in the House of the Lord For Ever

This psalm opened with the proud, joyous statement, "The Lord is my Shepherd."

Now it closes with the equally positive, buoyant affirmation, "And I will dwell in the house of the Lord for ever."

Here is a sheep so utterly satisfied with its lot in life, so fully contented with the care it receives, so much at home with the shepherd that there is not a shred of desire for a change.

Conversely, on the shepherd's side, there has developed a great affection and devotion to his flock. He would never think of parting with such sheep. Healthy, contented, productive sheep are his delight and profit. So strong now are the cords between them that it is in very truth forever.

The word "house" used here in the poem has a wider meaning than most people attach to it. Normally we speak of the house of the Lord as the sanctuary, church, or meeting place of God's people. In one sense David may have had this in mind. And, of course, it is pleasant to think that one would always delight to be found in the Lord's house. But actually, what is referred to by "house" is the family or household or flock of the good shepherd. The sheep is so deeply satisfied with the flock to which it belongs, with the ownership of this particular shepherd, that it has no wish whatsoever to change.

There is the "inner" consciousness, which can be very distinct and very real, of Christ's presence in our lives, made evident by His gracious Holy Spirit within.

Sometimes I feel we Christians should be more like this. We should be proud to belong to Christ. Why shouldn't we feel free to boast to others of how our Shepherd is? How glad we should be to look back and recall all the amazing ways in which He has provided for our welfare. We should delight to describe, in detail, the hard experiences through which He has brought us. And we should be eager and quick to tell of our confidence in

Christ. We should be bold to state fearlessly that we are so glad we are His. By the contentment and serenity in our lives we should show what a distinct advantage it is to be a member of His "household," of His flock.

. . . .

There is one other beautiful and final sense in which the psalmist was speaking as a sheep. It is found in the Amplified Old Testament, where the meaning of this last phrase is, "I will dwell in the presence of the Lord forever."

My personal conviction is that this is the most significant sentiment that David had in his heart as he ended this hymn of praise to divine intelligence.

Not only do we get the idea of an ever-present Shepherd on the scene, but also the concept that the sheep wants to be in full view of his owner at all times.

In our Christian lives and experience, the same idea and principle applies. For when all is said and done on the subject of a successful Christian walk, it can be summed up in once sentence: "Live ever aware of God's presence."

There is the "inner" consciousness, which can be very distinct and very real, of Christ's presence in our lives, made evident by His gracious Holy Spirit within. It is He who speaks to us in distinct and definite ways about our behavior. For our part, it is a case of being sensitive and responsive to that inner voice.

There can be a habitual awareness of Christ within me, empowering me to live a noble and richly rewarding life in cooperation with Him. As I respond to Him and move in harmony with His wishes I discover life becomes satisfying and worthwhile. It acquires great serenity and is made an exciting adventure of fulfillment as I progress in it. This is made possible as I allow His gracious Spirit to control, manage, and direct my daily decisions. In fact, I should deliberately ask for His direction, even in minute details.

Then there is the wider but equally thrilling awareness of God all around me. I live surrounded by His presence. I am an open person, an open individual, living life open to His scrutiny. He is conscious of every circumstance I encounter. He attends me with care and concern that I belong to Him. And this will continue through eternity. What an assurance!

I shall dwell in the presence (in the care of) the Lord forever.

Bless His name.

I am the good shepherd:
the good shepherd giveth his life
for the sheep.

I am the good shepherd,
and know my sheep, and am known
of mine.

—John 10:11, 14

Know ye that the LORD he is God: it is he that hath made us,
and not we ourselves; we are his people, and the sheep of his pasture.

—Psalm 100:3

"I will feed my flock, and I will cause them to lie down," saith the Lord God.

—Ezekiel 34:15

For the Lamb at the
center of the throne
will be their
shepherd;
he will lead them
to springs of
living water.
And God will
wipe away
every tear
from their
eyes.

—Revelation 7:17

Jesus said, "Fear not, little flock; for it is your Father's good pleasure to give you the kingdom."

—Luke 12:32

We thy people and sheep of thy pasture will give thee thanks for ever: we will show forth thy praise to all generations.

—Psalm 79:13